CORSICA
MARE É MONTE AND SARDINIA

Stephen Platt

www.leveretpublishing.com

Corsica: Mare é Monte and Sardinia
First published - November 2024
Published by Leveret Publishing
56 Covent Garden, Cambridge, CB1 2HR, UK

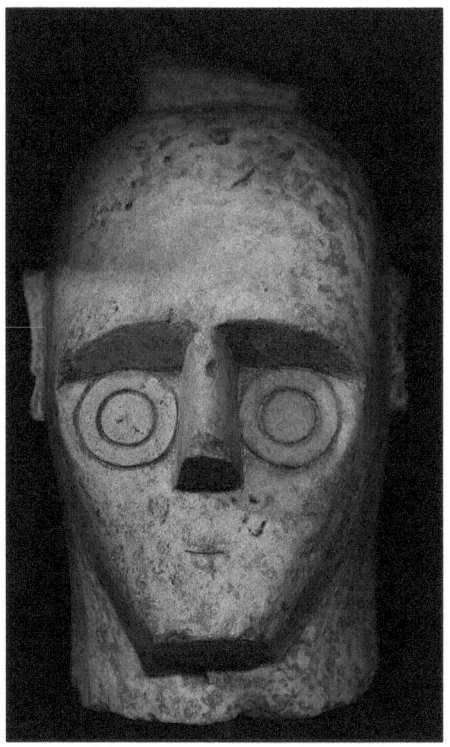

Giganti di Mont'e Prama Sardinia

ISBN 978-1-912460-70-0

© Stephen Platt 2024

All rights reserved. No part of this publication may be reproduced, stored in a retrieval system or transmitted in any form by any means, electronic, mechanical, photocopying, recording or otherwise, except brief extracts for the purpose of review, without the written permission of the publisher.

MARE É MONTE 2024

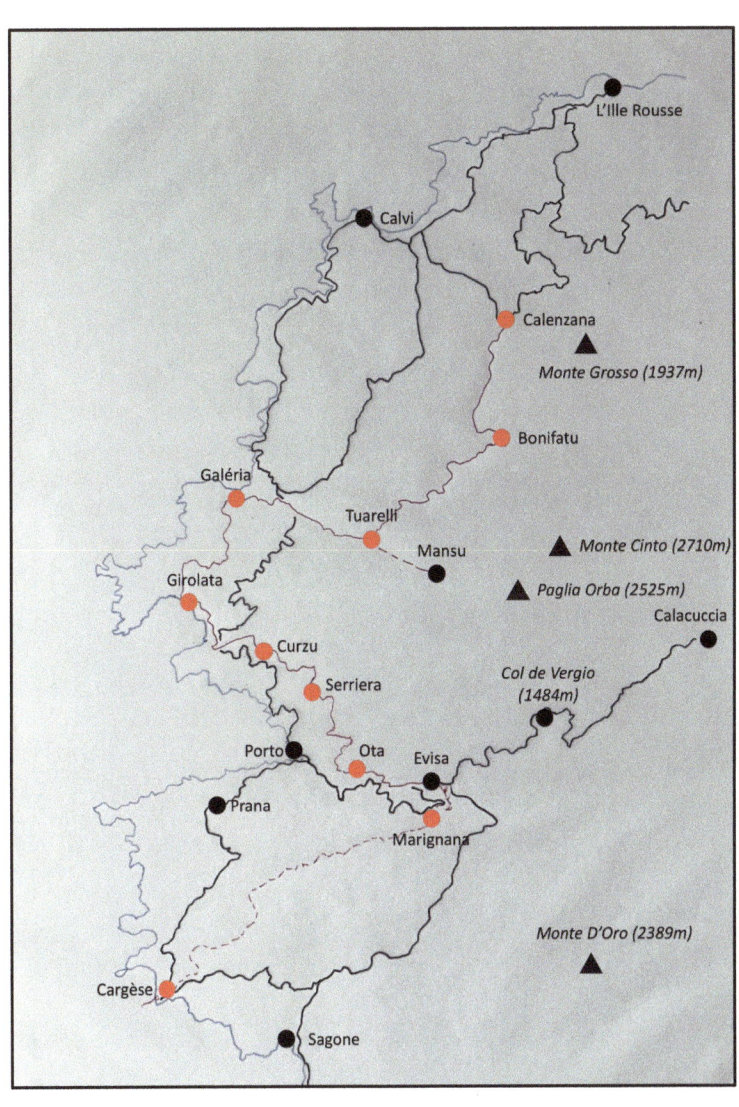

Days 1-2 The Journey

Thursday-Friday 19-20 September

It was sunny and warm in London, and I had dinner at the Mediterranean in Berwick Street, Soho, where a nice, young waiter served me vegetarian moussaka. My room in Eversholt Street near Euston Station was hot and the street noisy, so I had to close the windows to sleep; nevertheless, I had a good night, the only issue was cramp in my calves.

I awoke an hour later than planned, so no time for a shower before a brisk walk to St Pancras and a crowded concourse and full Eurostar train to Lille. There is a delightfully short walk from the Eurostar station, Lille Europe, to Lille Flanders and the onward train to Marseille. I ordered coffee and croissant in the same cafe I went to last year, and sat in warm autumn sunshine and watched the world go by.

Choosing lunch from a huge menu on a computer screen at the Pokawa

Leaving Marseille

bar in the station was an experience. In Marseille I followed signs for the port, which took me a more pleasant and interesting way than last time, when the main road cut through a seedy part of town. This time, I walked along an avenue of shops with views of the old city walls and the port, past the Hotel de Ville and on to the Old Port and promenade. Pink limestone walls tower above the sheltered harbour and the marina was jammed with yachts. Some of the restaurants along the promenade were open, but most were still shuttered, and would open later for dinner. I passed the harbour light house and reached the new waterfront. This part of the city is dominated by the white limestone of the Cathedral. It was a mile or so to the Gare Marina and the ferry terminal is so unassuming I nearly missed it again like I did last year.

The shuttle bus to the boat was crowded, and I jumped over cases to reach the one remaining seat. But everything went smoothly, and I passed the points I remembered from the epic last year when I nearly missed the ferry. What a nightmare.

The cabin was fine and the loos and shower clean and modern. I went on deck and then went for a shower and shaved while it was quiet before

Arriving at Port de L'Ile Rousse, Northern Corsica

going to the bar and buying a beer to have with the salad bowl I'd bought in Marseille. I ate on deck on a vacant bench, most of the passengers having gone inside now we'd left port and it had got dark and chilly. A good night and only slightly aware of the gentle movement of the ship.

Tour de L'Ile Rousse, Genoese 1530-1620

Day 3 Calenzana to Bonifatu

Saturday 21 September

I awoke naturally without the blast on the loudspeaker I was expecting and dressed quickly then the steep stairs to the car deck and walking off into the tiny Port de L'Île-Rousse (Red Island, from the colour of the rock.). It's early still and the sun is just coming up over the Genoese Tower and lighthouse on the headland to the east. I have time for a delicious cafe au lait and croissant in the harbour cafe while waiting for Michelle's taxi to Calenzana.

I remember little of Calenzana from 2001, only that Scharlie found the walk up through the maquis hot. I get some cash out of the ATM and buy a baguette sandwich for lunch in the Boulangerie and set off up the steep cobbled street and the Oratoire de St Antoine de Padoue. As soon as I leave the confines of the village I stop and change into shorts and t-shirt.

Oratoire de Saint Antoine de Padoue, Calenzana

Boulangerie and cafe

Torra - road to start of GR20 and Mare e Monte

There were other people on the trail, all doing the GR20 and all faster than me. But after the turn off to Bonifatu, there were no other walkers. I am finding it tough, unaccustomed to the weight of the pack and the heat, but I am going steadily to the col. I can look to my left and see the faint line of the trail to Arghioa and on to Refuge d'Ortu di u Piobbu, the first stop on the GR20.

The hillside is all green, clothed in dwarf elder and velvet ash, olive and strawberry trees with ripe pink fruit, which I pick and eat as I walk, having discovered that they were edible on my phone. They leave tiny seeds between my teeth which I find I'm spitting out for ages. There is also a bush with enticing myrtle-like berries that proved to be a mock privet and which were poisonous. There are signs of old forest fires with blackened trees, which is why they close the trails at times of fire risk in high summer.

The trail joins a forest road, which descends gently, contouring down the valley side. The Figarella river can be glimpsed at the foot of the slope, and houses and farmstead dot the wooded slopes and wild, grotesque rock formations rear up above the trail. The overhanging sandstone cliffs have been eroded into alien forms only rarely seen in horror movies which I

Junction with GR20

Strawberry tree (Arbutus unedo) high suger content and antioxidents

Disturbing rock formations near bridge over River Figarella

find surprisingly disturbing.

I reach the bridge and stop half an hour for lunch and take off my boots and eat most of my sandwich. Various old men pass over the bridge with small baskets. I think they must have been mushrooming in the forest, as it had rained recently and it is that time of the year.

From here, the trail followed the right bank of the river over jagged rocks and seemingly endless zigzags to reach the road and the final mile to the Auberge de la Foret, where I am to spend the night. The forest of Bonifatu (blessed place in Corsican) is a haven for wildlife and the great stands of Corsican or Laricio Pine (Pinus nigra) rising 40 metres, maritime pine, pygmy cedar, stone pine and brambles. At the bottom of the ravine, by the side of the tumbling river, there are the remains of a large ruined concrete house.

I arrive at L'Auberge de la Forêt. This is a popular destination, and there are lots of cars and people on terraces. My host is most welcoming, and the room superb with its own shower and toilet. I make tea, change and saunter down to the river. A family with small children and a pet goat were crossing the suspension bridge as I arrived. A man was planted in the

Typical rocky path

Cascade on path to Bonifatu

Ruin next to River Figarella

Suspension bridge at Bonifatu

middle of the bridge taking photographs. I waited a bit to see if he would move, then set off, trying not to bounce the ginger Pekingese with him into the torrent. He looked a bit put out, but I got passed safely and clambered over the rocks to a deep pool and dangled my feet in the icy water. Other braver people were dipping under but only for a minute as the sun had gone in and it was no longer hot. A shower and shave and a sleep before an excellent vegetable soup followed by a very filling penne pasta in a mushroom cream sauce. The bed was hard and the pillow too thin and it was a long night.

River figarella below Auberge de Foret

Day 4 Bonifatu to Tuarelli

Sunday 22 September

Breakfast at seven, and away by 7.45 having made a pumpernickel sandwich for lunch, plus half a chocolate brownie from last night. It was grey and chilly starting out and I wore my duvet but was soon warmed up on the endless zigzags. This path would be delightful if I was younger. But today I have to grit my teeth and keep plodding upwards. A Frenchman passed me going easily and was quickly out of sight.

The Corsican pines rise majestically, there are ferns growing in rocky crevices, and pink cyclamen poking through the pine needles. This high there are fungi, deep red Russula, that have escaped the elderly mushroom hunters, but there are other hunters about because I can hear the crack of their guns in the near distance. I pass the ruin of the chalet of Prince Pierre, Bonaparte's nephew. It is a large stone ruin and the fallen walls are moss covered and there are holm oak growing through the floor. There is a

Prince Bonaparte chalet

Stately Corsican pine (Pinus nigra)

View of Calvi from Bocca dei l'Erbeghiolo (1200m)

separate building that may have been the servants' quarters. I imagine parties coming here on mule back and hunting the wild boar.

The path ascends through great stands of stately Corsican pines, Finally I sense the tree cover thinning, and see the crest of the ridge to my left beginning to ease. The path suddenly reaches the coll. What a relief! There is a view down to Calvi, and I can see the airport runway. I stop and take off my boots and drink lots of water. The path is now downhill through or along the flat to the next Boca, from where there is a tricky descent crossing loose rocks through rough maquis fountain grass, Russian Thistle and mountain ash. It's important not to fall here.

At midday, I stop on a rocky slab and eat my lunch, the baguette from yesterday. There's a long walk downhill along a forest trail to Boca Lucca and another short rest. Looking back up to the rocky ridge at the head of the cirque the slopes are covered in holm oak and pine and I can see no sign of the path I've followed from the col. Onward I can look down into the Fangu Valley and I speed up on the easy downslope.

The gîte in Tuarelli is abandoned and looks most sad and unloved, with lots of mess and rubbish cluttering the covered patios. I retrace my steps

River Fangu Tuarelli

to the road and cross the bridge and look down 50 feet to the deep rock pools that look inviting, and I wonder if anyone has ever jumped from the bridge. I start walking on the road. It's about four miles to Mansu, and I'm hoping for a lift, a Swiss couple stop and rearrange all the clutter in the car to make space in the back for me. I find the address on Google Maps and it's another three miles beyond Mansu and I would never have managed to walk it, but the Swiss most kindly take me all the way.

Guy and Veronique, my hosts, are most welcoming. The room is nice. And because it's Sunday everywhere is closed, and Veronique offers to make supper. I have a shower, wash any clothes and have a rest till dinner is ready – courgette and tuna quiche and boiled eggs with a mustard mayonnaise sauce followed by a chocolate pot. Veronique suggests her husband can give me a lift in the morning.

Pont de Tuvarelli

Day 5 Tuvarelli to Galéria

Monday 23 September

I chat with Guy and Veronique over breakfast. She's a good cook, and has made brownies, which she said I could take for lunch, homemade marmalade and fresh bread. Guy was in the French army like his father, and his job had been maintaining helicopters. It was difficult moving around when I was young, he said. He met Veronique in the Bourgogne and worked fourteen years as a taxi driver in Lyon before moving to Corsica and his grandfather's land. You ask yourself, what are you doing with your life? You make choices. They have been in this house 26 years, and he has taken it from four bare walls and no roof to a delightful home with a pool. I like his style —black kitchen cabinets and wood floor and anthracite windows and doors. Veronique has lots of cats; I counted seven.

Guy talked about, Pasquale Paoli, the man who liberated Corsica from the Genoese. Paoli lived in London in exile and wrote the Corsica

Ponte Vechju, River Fangu

Constitution that, amongst other progressive ideas, gave votes to women and became a model for the American Constitution. Paoli had stayed in London refusing the French offer to reinstate him as a puppet governor. Guy drove fast on the bendy road. I had contemplated walking back to Tuarelli along the path on the riverside, but was glad I hadn't as it seemed so far.

The rocky path from Tuarelli follows the river through maquis of mock privet and rock rose. After a mile or so the Ponte Vecchiu comes into view framed by a large red gum eucalyptus. It's an elegant single arch spanning the river at a narrowing between rock bluffs and there is a lorry gingerly crossing. A couple are getting ready to swim as I climb down to the river, careful not to slip on the smooth rock chute. I strip off and paddle. Later I regret not going in and swimming. It wasn't that cold, and you get used to it. There is a stretch along the road to Fangu where there is a restaurant on the junction and half a dozen motorbikes were drawn up on the roadside. People were lunching on pork and chips. I stopped for a macchiato, coffee and lemonade.

A hundred metres along the road, just over the bridge, the path climbs

Ponte Vechju

La Ciucciarella restaurant, Fangu

Galéria

and then runs parallel to the road. The path goes on a good while, and I stop at a water tower and put on my anorak because there's a brief rainstorm. I get a view of the Fangu Delta and a long sandy beach. There is a steep bit past a ruin to get over the final bluff before Galleria comes into view – a sheltered bay and a pebble beach. The path doesn't give up though, and it's demanding, but I can see the end, and I'm going well. I'm just congratulating myself in not having fallen when my right boot slides and I'm down on my bottom, no damage, apart from my pride.

I'm into the village. The grass terraces in the centre of the village form an intricate maze of low stone walls and dry drainage channels with olive and almond trees . At one time they must have provided the villagers with fresh vegetables, but they are no longer farmed in that way and are grazed by the odd cow or goat. It's quiet at this time of the day and there is an end of season feel. I use the sat nav to find my hotel. Platt, she says, with a knowing smile and shows me my room at the side on the ground floor.

I put on my trunks and go down to the beach, stride into the water, the beach shelves steeply, and I'm suddenly out of my depth, and don't dare swim out to the buoys, where a couple are swimming. I'm out of practice.

Terraces Galeriea

I was never a strong swimmer but used to be much braver when I was young, nevertheless, I'm in and getting wet.

I'm hungry but the restaurants are all closed. It's only 5:30 and some of them will open their doors in two and a half hours. So I go back to the hotel for a shower and a rest before venturing forth to the L'Aghja Nova restaurant near the church and order a steak kebab, thinking I might need the protein tomorrow, as it's a tough day with a steep 700m ascent. The stars are out on the way back to the hotel and the mountains black cut-out shapes rising out of the dark sea.

Beach Galeria

Day 6 Galéria to Girolata

Tuesday 24 September

The day started well. I was worried I wouldn't have enough cash for the next stage, but by spending five euros in the spa on nut bars I got 60 euros cash-back, and the post office was open at 8:30 so I managed to get another 300 Euros.

The path follows the river, climbing gently to a dam. The going is easy at first, then becomes more difficult with tricky scrambles over rockslides and smooth slabs, which might be a problem if it was wet. There were small ducks on the dam, and the water looked still and dark. I can see the ridge I'm aiming for at the head of the valley. Ancient olive and rock rose border the stream bed.

The path steepens, and I find it hard work, but manage to keep going as far as craggy lookout and a magnificent view of Galleria and the coast. I'm

Dam on Ruisseau de Tavulaghiu

not there yet and it's still a couple of hundred metres to the ridge. Gnarled blackened tree roots, clinging to and burrowing into the shallow red earth. The slope steepens, I'm pushing on my walking sticks for leverage.

Finally an oak tree at the at the crest bent over by the wind sweeping over the col from the sea to the south and signs for Girolata. Windswept on the south side; verdant to the north. The ridge slopes down at first and I take pleasure in the gentle effortless needed to advance. Then up through park land of giant oaks to a lunch stop of bread and tapenade and honey and jam. I take off my boots and rest my tired feet and arthritic toes. It feels nice to stop, if only for twenty minutes. I drink plenty of water. It's important to stay hydrated, since I'm lightheaded enough with the exertion

The ridge is delightfully rocky and precipitous, with great views north and south. The pale grey coastline appears as an archipelago of magical islands floating in a zephyr mist. There is maquis with sharp buckthorn, tennis ball bush and ephedra to negotiate. The path drops into low, hanging woodland of holm oak, enchanting. There is a weather station and I stop for a drink. The station is powered by solar panels and has a

Cairn

Holm oak Punta Literniccia (778m)

View down to Girolata

communication mast, sending data automatically. The ridge is much longer than I expected and rises to a second summit with a great view down to Girolata, before descending down a rocky headland to the Bocca. I have to take care here not to slip and fall. It seems a long way down, and the glimpses one has of the bay through the trees don't seem to make the sea get any nearer.

The path descends a gorge and finally reaches a level promenade that runs as far as the village. The cream coloured castle looks fairy tale, and I can see yachts anchored in the bay and pleasure boats ferrying in day trippers. I reach the gîte and I'm shown my room before sallying forth to explore along the beach. They are repairing the jetties with massive timbers that I think are Opepe from West Africa, a marine timber I used at Guilden Morden for two bridges.

Back at the gîte, I have a shower and shave and greet the three Norwegians I'd met earlier today. The women are sisters. They did the Mare e Monte six years ago and had come to do it again with their "little" brother. They go off to sample the wares of the beachside stalls, while I climb to the terrace restaurant to have a beer. It's six o'clock, and all the

Crest of the ridge

Entrance to village and Fortin de Girolata

Fortin de Girolata

Repairing jerries in Girolata, Gite Le Cormoran Voyageur in background

Prickly pear (Oportunia)

day trippers have left on their small ferries, and there are just a few people from the yachts coming in on inflatable dinghies for dinner. The main form of transport here seems to be mini Mokes or quad bikes, and the locals seem to travel around on these vehicles, pulling trailers.

I try to find a way to the castle, but it seems to be private and the way is closed, so I wander off down a lane into the country. There are all sorts of encampments and allotments in the fields and the place has a gypsy, anarchic air about it. The bright red prickly pear fruit looks ripe and inviting

I get to know my fellow guests over dinner, the three Norwegians, Chris and two sisters and a Swiss couple from Lucerne, Thomas and Marguerite. We talk about what we like about Corsica; we've all been here before and we talk about the GR 20, and why the Cirque de Solitude is closed. Thomas said because of an accident, when people died descending in the storm. Chris asked me what other big walks I'd done and I'd recommend. And I asked him where I should go in Norway, Far North he said, the Lofoten Islands or Tromso.

Girolata bay

Day 7 Girolata to Curzu

Wednesday 25 September

I woke with alarm when I found my phone hadn't charged. It seems that the charger is faulty, because I managed to charge with the battery. Breakfast was the usual coffee and homemade jams. I made a sandwich with the fig jam, pay and say goodbye, then a walk along the beach and join the cliff path that climbs quite high above the sea. It is narrow, precipitous and quite tricky and I took extreme care not to slip and fall.

The path descends to the beach at Tuara and I think I have it to myself until I find that there are three kayakers camping under a tarp stretched between bleached driftwood spars. I strip off and get into the sea. It's warm after the initial shock, the sun is strong enough to dry me off, so I don't need to use my towel.

I make a move and set off on the path to the Col de la Croix –

Cliff path to Tuara

Tuara beach

Rideg above Bocca a Croce

straightforward, if a little demanding. What was extraordinary was the dozens of people descending from the col. I wondered if they were going to Girolata, and if they'd all make it, since the average age must have been in the mid 70s. There is a snack bar at the Col where I stop for a coffee and orange juice.

The ridge above the bar climbs 400 meters in a steady, continuous slope that's more like an English mountain going straight up without the Corsican zigzags. At first I like it because it feels more efficient, but as my legs tire, I miss the change and the mini rest the zigs provide. But I'm getting there and after the peak the ridge levels out flat to a rocky escarpment that also needs care. Then a final ascent of a rocky bluff and I'm at the massive holm oak at the saddle and can stop for a late lunch on my fig sandwich.

The descent to the Curzu takes an hour, and then I'm at the fountain below the church and the slope down to the road. The gite opens up after I've been sitting a while, and I shower and wash my clothes and have a drink on the terrace before dinner, I chat with two nice German cyclists from Bremen and Berlin. They did the GR French 20 some years ago. There is time before dinner and I walk up to the fountain and sit with my

Ancient holm oak on saddle above Curzu

back to the church wall in the evening sun and watch the light and cloud shadows move across the mountains to the south. The buttresses and cliffs of Capo d'Orto glow golden in the setting sun.

There is a girl sitting reading on the wall above, who, it turns out, is also staying at the gite. Dominique, our host, has excelled himself with a delicious vegetable soup followed by cannelloni with cheese and spinach and a separate pan full of veal in a creamy sauce, then a little cheese, and finally, chocolate ice cream. I tell him it's the best food any gite has served so far, and he seems delighted. The girl is in her early 20s and is backpacking around Europe. She did Courchevel this winter, and now she's doing Corsica. She has a job lined up as a barmaid but is doing some of the Mare e Monte before she starts. She wants to know about the GR 20, and if it's dangerous. The weather can change quickly and ideally, you should keep your pack to eight kilograms. She looks alarmed. Hers is obviously much heavier. She looks strong and young and says she's going all the way to Galleria tomorrow.

Capu d'Ortu

Day 8 Curzu to Serriera

Thursday 26 September

It seemed a long night. Delightfully, there is abundant coffee and lots of milk and, what luxury, a jug of orange juice, freshly pressed. I'm away soon after eight and climbing the road from the gite to the church and on through the village. I'm already puffing like Thomas the Tank Engine. Mercifully, the gradient eases and I reach the path and begin the ascent proper.

It mentioned thorns in the maquis in the guide, but the way was clear, contouring round the hillside and rising to a mini peak in woodland. Today, it's cloudy and breezy, and although the south wind is warm, it's better than hot sun and still air. Fritillary, graylings, common blue, swallowtails and small tortoiseshell butterflies and the continual background sound of grasshoppers. Views down to the sea and due east to the main spine of the island that the GR 20 follows where the mountains look dark and forbidding, silhouetted against the threatening sky. But I longed to be there

Drinking fountain below the church at Curzu

Curzu

Path down to Serriera

on the ridge, getting high, rather than struggling down here in the foothills.

Now I have to focus and keep plodding up and on, finally cresting out and then descending to the dry ravine, where I stop for a drink from my bottle. On the way down, I meet a party of five women. They're French, doing the Mare e Monte in the opposite direction. I ask whether the way from Ota is still closed, but they don't seem to know.

There is another ascent to cross a second ridge. I'd imagined this would be a nice, easy day, but it's proving tough, just shorter. There is a sudden stampede of hooves and the undergrowth shakes as I disturb a wild pig or boar that crashes downhill through the undergrowth. Finally, I reach the col above the village and stop at a low wall and have the apricot sandwich I made at breakfast. It's fairly low down and hot in the village, and I find the auberge and book for supper before ringing Regine and getting into the gite. I have a room to myself, and I have a shower and shave and make tea.

The villages are a strange mixture of abandonment and recent renovation and activity, with a few local farmers hanging on and newcomers coming in and buying second homes. Tomorrow and the day

Serriera

Eglise Sanat Maria Serriera

Abandoned houses Serriera

after are bigger days and I wonder how I'll get on if I found today hard. One thing at a time. I mean to control my breathing better, but, as the consultant explained, the chronic kidney disease means they get out of breath easily.

It's still early and warm, and I walk to the beach. Regine said it was two or three kilometres and would only take 25 minutes. But it seems longer. The road from Serriera joins the main Calvi to Porto road for a bit before turning off to the beach. This is some kind of nature reserve. There are cars and a few people on the beach. It's pebbly, and I get into my trunks and wade in. The beach shelves suddenly and within three meters I'm out of my depth and swimming. The water is warm and there is a strong surf running, and I don't stay in long, but it's most refreshing and reviving. I ask a couple for a lift, and they take me to the Serriera turning and it seems quicker walking back and I'm soon at the gite.

The restaurant is fascinating. It's housed in an olive press, and the wooden basin, stone wheel and supporting timbers now form part of the bar. There is a great menu, and rather than have the standard sheet fair of cannelloni, I opt for magret de canard in a honey sauce with a sanglier

Plage de Bussaghlia

terrine starter and a fig tart for dessert. The helpings are large and I'm over-faced and have to leave part of the main course.

Olive Press restaurant Serraria

Gite d'Etape L'Alivi

Looking east to main ridge

Day 9 Serraria to Ota

Friday 27 September

Breakfast was in the restaurant with nice coffee, and I was away soon after eight. A couple of miles of gently ascending forestry road, then the track branches off up the hillside, and there begins an unrelenting ascent that seems to go on and on. I reach a rocky promontory, thinking I'm there, but there is still another 150 meters of gruelling ascent to reach the col. The black and white plumage of a bird decorates the path and there is lots of wild boar action. Interestingly they root at the side of the path and leave a narrow track undamaged.

I leave my pack at the col and walk back to Capu San Petru (913m) along the delightful ridgeway. It's much nearer than I expected, and the summit is a rocky pile just a few meters higher than the path. Some of the trees are dying and are covered in 'old-man's beard' lichen. I follow the ridgeway in the other direction, and at a sign for the Bergerie de Larata, I

Capu San Petru (913m)

Capu d'Orta

Old man's beard lichen

branch off on the way to Ota. The guide said this was tricky and needed care, but there was a brand new sign and lots of orange markers.

I drop down into the Ruisseau de Vitrone ravine. The way is narrow, rocky and difficult, and the orange red walls of the ravine overhang. I'm finding it very hard going. I'm tired after the long ascent and I am trying not to fall. I nearly come to grief as my toe catches under a rock and I pitch forward and stagger a few steps trying to keep my balance. Towards the end of the ravine I stop where the path crosses a tiny stream and dangle my sore feet in the water and rub Arnica on the bruise on my shin where I caught my boot. It's most reviving. I refill my water bottle, have my last nut bar and press on. It's really hot now, and I put my handkerchief under my cap to stop my neck burning and apply factor 50 liberally to my ears and face.

I've been practicing deeper breathing through my nose all day rather than gasping for breath through my mouth, and it seems to be working. It makes me feel less frenetic and anxious to get the oxygen in. And although I find it difficult at first, I press on. I am usually is unaware of smell but the scents of Corsica are particularly strong today. Thyme, mint and marjoram,

Sentier Ghineparu Pianu

Ravine di Ruisseau de Vitrone

Overhanging cliffs

the dry smell of the earth and the rock, the faint smell of boar shit, of rock rose and dry flower heads. It's such a medley that it's impossible to differentiate the different scents.

The ravine seems endless, and I expect the path to ease, but in fact, it maintains its challenging nature all the way to Ota as it traverses up and down the mountainside, moving east up the valley, until finally I am there.

A Frenchman staying in the gite gave me the lowdown and found me a towel and I had a lovely shower and washed my sweaty clothes. Time to kill till dinner, so I walk through the village to a shop where I buy almonds, an apple and a lovely juice drink of orange, carrot and lemon. Then back to the gite for tea and write my journal.

Village of Ota

Day 10 Ota to Evisa

Saturday 28 September

I awoke naturally at six. The dorm is full, and I got up quietly and sat on the balcony and watched the dawn appear. The mountains are black silhouettes against the lightening sky illuminated by stars and a crescent moon. From the centre of the village where the lights are on, there is a bubble of voices, and the sounding of the clock for seven. Maybe it's children waiting for the school bus. It's like the bubbling of a stream, constant, mellifluous, occasionally rising distinctly with a male voice. I see movement in the large building that I think is the restaurant. The burble of children's voices has quickened with the bell but is still there as the sky lightens. The first car glides silently through the village. Above the rock wall of Capu d'Ota rises vertically and is crowned by a huge square block that seems poised to fall but is said to be held in place by three celestial chains.

After breakfast I set off through the village, past the fountain I couldn't

Ota in the evening light

Typical Corsica village house

Rivière de Porto

see yesterday because of all the parked cars, and then the snack bar where the children had been waiting for the school bus. A strong smell of mint and thyme as the road becomes a track. There is a battered gate with a sign saying closed because of landslides. I had asked about the trail from the various people I'd met. The majority said that the last part of the gorge beyond the third bridge was still closed. But the lady in the gite in Ota had said that with care I'd get through alright. And I'd met two young Frenchmen in the ravine who were doing the Mare e Monte in the opposite direction and who had said the difficult section was just a few metres. So I pressed on, imagining I'd be able to climb over the difficult bit. Down to the riverbank and a rocky path to the first bridge, with its delicate Genoese arch.

There has been a mini slide just beyond the bridge, but the path is soon regained and rises steadily. The gorge narrows as it gets higher, the red walls crowding in on the blue band of the river. I reach the road bridge and beginning of the Spelunca Gorge proper. There are one or two other difficult passages where the path has disappeared under fallen rock. But this isn't the main landslide yet. This is after the third bridge. I'm tired after the

Pont Génoise

hard day yesterday, and my legs feel wobbly and unsteady, and I hope I don't fall. I won't be insured if I have an accident, because the assessor will discover that the path was closed and I shouldn't have been here.

The gorge is dramatic and quite splendid – red sandstone cliffs framed by majestic pines and the sound of the tumbling water. I reach the third bridge. The Zaglia bridge is an engineering marvel and spans the Tavulella, a tributary of the main river, and without it would have been difficult to get across when the river was in spate. All these paths between villages, some of which the Mare e Monte follows, were for transhumance of animals, bringing them from mountain grazing in the winter. Today, it would have been possible to boulder hop or to ford the stream, but in winter, the water would be much higher.

Now begins the hardest part of the day as the path climbs the side of the gorge in endless zigzags. At first it is well-made, then I come to the slide and have to use my hands and climb and take care. There is a large, poised boulder that overhangs the paths that I have to lean out on and place my feet carefully. But I get across all right and continue upwards. On and on, trying to control my breathing, trying to ignore the sharp pains in

Pont Génoise

my knees from the long descent yesterday.

I feel I'm getting there as the path begins to ease, but there are still a dozen zigzags before I finally reach the road and walk through Tumbes to Evisa and find the cafe where I bought sandwiches last year and order lunch, vegetable panini, fries and orange presse. I have a decision to make, whether to continue on to Marignana where I'm booked into the gite, and to complete the 21 miles to Cargese, or to cancel Marignana and get a lift to Cargese. The gite at E Casa is closed so the last two stages from Marignana to Cargese have to be run together. I did them last year on the Mare a Mare trek by taking a taxi back up to Revinda on the second day. That was uphill in the other direction, so I had reasoned that since it was mainly downhill I'd be able to do it in one hit. But now I felt I'd had enough. It was nice just stopping. After all I'd done it before.

The Evisa taxi, the barman recommends can't come till seven, so I cast around until I finally find someone who says she'll ask someone to ring me back. It's an hour and a half wait and will cost 150 euros, but I'm glad I have a plan that will get me to Cargese.

Corse goats

Start of Spelunca gorge

Road bridge at start of Spelunca gorge

Pont Zaglia

Evisa

Day 11 Cargese

Sunday 29 September

A very long lie in and then a big breakfast. I boil an egg to take for lunch and decide to walk to the Tour Génoise de Cargèse at the end of Omigna promontory. It's five or six kilometres and should take an hour or so according to Google. It's a steep descent on the road to the beach, and I remember doing it the first day of the Mare a Mare walk last year.

The road ends and the track begins. I can't believe how tired my legs feel, but it's great to be walking without the pack weighing me down. The tower has been renovated, and there is now a steel staircase and a stone spiral stair to the circular top, where there is a new a view back to Cargèse and down into the crashing waves. It's windy today, and there is a sea running.

I sit with my back against the low stone wall and eat my boiled egg and

Tour Génoise de Cargèse at the end of Omigna promontory

Rock near tower

On the top of the Tour Génoise

baguette and watch the other visitors. A couple of women are lounging on the wall enjoying a chat.

It seemed quicker on the way back, and I stopped at the beach and paddled in the sea, it being too rough for me to go in swimming. I got a lift up the hill with a lovely couple from Ajaccio who dropped me at the hotel where I had tea and paid up and checked arrangements for tomorrow. It turned out I hadn't booked the hotel in Santa Teresa and had to find another. I went out to eat and had gambas and a glass of wine and then an early bed.

Tomorrow I head for Sardinia having decided to spend a few days there resting and exploring.

Tour Génoise

Day 12 Cargese to Bonifacio and Santa Teresa

Monday 30 September

Monday, a dawn start and a couple of minutes wait for the Cyril's taxi, and then off down the endless curves to Ajaccio. Cyril has an 18-year-old son at college in Corte studying accountancy. He points out the sites and views with a 'tres joie' for each of them.

There was just time to buy a coffee and croissant before boarding the coach. There are a number of foreigners on board – a father backpacking with a young son, two Canadian ladies who smoked at every stop. Those going to Bonifacio were dropped off in Figari, where there was a minibus waiting to complete the journey to Bonifacio. The old boy drove quite fast. You need to be a good driver in Corsica.

Bonifacio is beautiful. It's the oldest city in Corsica. Its cliff-top citadel, the Bastion de l'Etendard, dates from the 9th-century. The Haut Ville and

Bonifacio harbour

fortress are built on a long finger promontory that runs west parallel with the coast forming a long sheltered harbour. The sunny marina at the eastern end of the bay is lined with promenade restaurants. I picked one at which to stop for lunch. I try my luck again with soup de poisson but regret not ordering a plate of small fried fish like whitebait that I see on my neighbour's plate.

There is a stiff climb up to the Ville Haute and the Citadel. It's an amazingly fortified town, and I vow to learn more of its history when I get back.

I'd imagined I'd done all my climbing on the Mare e Monte, but this climb taxed my tired limbs. Wandering about the narrow alleys and finding the main church for a brief rest on a pew contemplating the almighty then a wander back past dozens and dozens of restaurants. A refreshing tea in the cafe next to the boarding gate, then a wait to board, and a wait on deck in the hot sun. It's just an hour to Sardinia and I found a seat and settled in and relaxed and took off my boots.

Entering the long narrow harbour in Santa Teresa de Gallura the ferry swung round and reversed in. I had found an apartment close to both the

La Haute Ville (the Upper city) Bonifacio, Église Sainte Marie Majeure

ferry and the bus terminal, and it was a just short walk up the hill and a series of WhatsApp messages to get into the Angelique. It was spacious and pleasant and despite being on the road, it was quiet. After a shower and change, I set off to explore and find the bus station.

Unfortunately, I set the phone to car mode and Google Maps took us all round the houses on the one way system, and I walked four to five times what we needed to. I had a nice chat to an English couple from Thornbury near Bristol in the bus station who were waiting on a bench for an 8:30pm bus to La Maddalena. They have been exploring the island and talk about the archeological sites they'd visited.

I talked to men in the cafe and find out that the airport bus stopped yesterday and the timetable had changed on the first of October, but I can get an ordinary bus at 9:35 to Olbia and change for the airport. The couple recommended a restaurant run by a Californian but on the way to the centre, I passed a wine bar that looked good and went in and ordered spaghetti with pumpkin sauce and a glass of Rose frizzante.

La Haute Ville

Citadel built in the 9th century by Boniface II of Tuscany i

La forteresse de Bonifacio at the western end of the promontory

SARDINIA

Day 13 Santa Teresa de Galuria to La Caletta

Tuesday 1 October

A short walk to the bus and a coffee and croissant in the cafe while waiting to board. The drivers are like gods of the road here. They drive so precisely on these narrow, twisting roads and go down streets in villages that I would be nervous about in a small car, and then turn in spaces that seem much too small for a bus. The end of the line is a nondescript bus stop on an undistinguished street In Olbia. Everyone got off and stood waiting, so I joined them, and five minutes later, the bus to the airport arrived.

It's a tiny airport, and there is a separate hall for car hire. The man at the Noleggiare desk was nice, and I hired an automatic which cost a bit more and set off with my phone linking to the screen through Apple play. The speed limits are low here, and the traffic is sedate, so driving isn't a problem. I drove to the coastal resort of Budoni because I liked the name.

Palau Galuria

It's so much more developed here than in 2006 when I came last, and all the villas look similar – pink render on block work with shallow red tile roofs. Sardinia seems quite unlike Corsica. It's lower for a start, and less mountainous, and consequently less green, less treed and more built up. But it's more than that, it seems that planning regulation, or the application of it, is much less strict here than in Corsica. So settlements look more anarchic and scruffier. There are many more advertising signs and visual clutter. Settlements in Corsica seem to sit comfortably in the environment and housing a generally renovated older property with well-cut masonry walls. Here, villas seem to have been plonked, higgledy-piggledy, with little consideration for their setting. I can feel myself reacting badly and am trying not to be so negative and just accept and enjoy the difference.

I'm hungry and spot a place on Google that looks like it's a nature reserve near the beach. It's a wonderful restaurant built under the pine trees that give shade. The tree trunks are part of the structure. At first you don't notice them. Then you realise that the dark columns holding up the roof are living trees. The food is equally amazing. They must have a fantastic chef. I have ravioli, which comes on a long, narrow dish with a

Shardana restaurant Pineta Sant'Anna

pasta laid out in a line with delicious dips of different sauces. It's astonishing how many different tastes can be crowded into such a simple dish.

I need to find somewhere to stay. There seems to be lots of choice. The cheaper flats, however, are some distance from the beach, and I can see they would involve a climb of a few blocks through housing. Finally, I found a beachfront apartment in La Caletta that said it had a sea view and was only 50 meters from the beach. So I went to look at it and booked it on Booking.com on my phone. The host texted me to say that, unfortunately, the apartment I booked was unavailable because the previous guests had damaged the hob in the kitchen, but that the ground floor apartment was available and just the same. So I agreed to take it.

I went shopping for some groceries and water in the local Craic supermarket, by which time, the man's brother, Giovanni, had arrived with the keys. My first impression of the flat was disappointing. There was no view, and it was rather spartan. I think I was influenced by my negative thoughts about Sardinia its over development, I was also feeling ill and lightheaded. I had a cough, my ears were blocked, and I had a headache and had begun to shake with cold. But I didn't allow myself to whinge and

La Calletta

had a lovely hot shower. Halfway through, I sneezed, and the sound of the splashing water increased dramatically as my ears cleared, I found the heater and made some food and began to feel better.

Spiaggia la Caletta

Day 14 La Caletta to Orosei

Wednesday 2 October

I had a good night and went shopping for coffee and milk and had a delicious breakfast of melon and peach salad with Yogurt. This isn't half bad, I thought, as I changed into trunks and headed for the beach with one of the garden chairs.

The water is warm and the sea calm and shallow, and I went for a swim and then sat in the weak sunshine. This feels like the end of the season. The beach isn't crowded and there are just a few swimmers. I had taken a plastic folding chair from the apartment. It was a bit heavy, but worth it. I sat and wrote my journal and listened to Broken Shore by Peter Temple on audiobooks. It was chilly after three, so I lay down on the sand where it was warmer, and soaked up the afternoon rays of October

I had a late lunch of scrambled egg and tomato, and as I set off south to

Spiaggia la Caletta

Via San Giacomo Orosei

Chiesa del Rosario Orosei

Chiesa del Rosario Orosei

Bar di Solinas Anna maria Piazza del Popolo

Orosei the scenery changed dramatically. You notice the difference immediately. Umbrella pines, neat olive groves, new stone walls and a field newly sown with olive whips. It's still dry, but beautiful. I imagine it much greener in spring. I realised my first negative impression of Sardinia of the area between Santa Teresa and Olbia seen from the moving bus gave a false impression of the whole island and there was much more to Sardinia.

In Orosei, I climbed the narrow streets heading for the historic centre and found somewhere to park. I had a drink in a cafe in front of the church. There were two young women with a baby boy. Then granddad arrived and lavished love on the child, carrying him around, which seemed to make the young mother a little nervous. Then dad arrived, looking about 19. Before I left I explored the narrow streets, admiring ancient forms. The old church is a wonderful, rambling, massive stone structure with a bell tower.

It seemed too early to drive back, so I decided to check out a spaggia I could see on Google. It proved to be a delightful area of pine woods bordering the sea with a freshwater lagoon between the dunes and the road. Rather than go back the same way, I decided to take a chance on

Stagno Pettrosu Osala

what looked like a track that wound 15 or 20 kilometres back to the main road. The tarmac surface soon disappeared, and I was on gravel, driving slowly. This is a deeply agricultural area, and various farms offer agro-tourism. There were views of limestone mountains to the south.

Views from agricultural track and SS125 highway

Day 15 La Caletta to Talana, Blue Zone and Nuora

Thursday 3 October

Going south on the national highway is quite different to the north of the island. It's entirely rural and looks beautiful after the rain last night. It's very forested with neat looking trees and olive groves. There seem to be very few settlements, only isolated farm states and occasional towns. The highway engineering is a marvel and they have recently replaced all the barriers. From high on a mountain road the motorway is a thin white line running beautifully straight down the central valley of Sardinia. Either side is green, wild, mucky on the hillsides, prickly pear, where it's dry, but beautifully laid out olive groves and vineyards. The olives have self-seeded and ancient, stately trees clothe the hillsides. My mood and feeling about Sardinia have changed completely. The Gennagentu massif must be a national park, given how pristine it looks.

At Nuoro, there is a tunnel which runs under the town, and Google

Bar in Talana

Maps shows the streets one is passing under. The road to Tomba de Gigantes leaves the autostrada and climbs into the hills. Both Sardinia and Southern Corsica are rich in bronze age archaeology. I realise later that I hadn't done my homework. I usually bone-up on a place and read about the local history, but I haven't. In fact Sardinia is littered with over 7000 nuraghe, megalithic stone round towers dating from 1900 to 700 BC, and hundreds of tomba de gigantes, sanctuaries and sacred wells. The tomba I had happened to see on the Google map was therefore just one of many sites I might have visited. There are cows pastured where Google says I've arrived, and a magnificent bull, but it starts to rain, there are no signs, and I retreat before I get soaked.

I continue along the mountain road towards Talana and Abraxas. It's a winding mountain road and the rest of the day is like this – switchback narrow roads with great views of the mountains shrouded in mist. This is a great motorbike country, and bikes that pass me would be having a great time if it wasn't raining so hard. I stop in Talana outside the Carrera bar and go in and order a hot chocolate. It's so thick, it's almost a mousse; totally delicious.

Tomba de Gigantes

I eat half of my cheese sandwich and set off in search of Blue Zone villages. Blue zones, of which there are five in the world, are places where there is a very high incidence of centenarians, identified by Dan Buettner from demographic data. Sardinia, specifically the mountainous area southeast of Nuoro, was the first to be identified. It was suggested that long life was due to lifestyle and a combination of physical activity, low stress, rich social interactions, a local whole-foods diet, and low disease incidence. I was skeptical and wondered if there really was sufficient evidence to justify the claims.

The nearest blue zone village on my route was Urzulie. It was interesting because it was so ordinary and unremarkable. Perhaps I expected more obvious, physical evidence of Blue Zone living. Perhaps I had in mind an idyllic, unspoiled medieval settlement with old men with moustaches and flat caps. Perhaps I didn't stay long enough to really learn anything.

Endless blues of the mountains, overlapping shades of grey as they recede into the distance and distant cliffs and deep gorges glimpsed through roadside trees and through mist shrouded mountainsides. I descend a deep gorge clothed in mist and stop in a lay by. The cliffs look

Blue zone village of Urzulie

impressive but the mist is too thick to take a decent photograph. From here, I head for Oleana and Nuoro via Dorgali. Nuoro is amazing. It straddles the mountain ridge and is huge; much bigger than I'd thought. Why anyone would want to put a city up here on these steep slopes is beyond me.

Google wants to take me back the way I've come, but I want to go north to regain the autopista, so I override Google's preference. It's a long way down lots of curves, but eventually I regain the flat land and the motorway. Back in La Caletta, I buy a fungi and truffle ravioli for supper and a dish of fresh anchovies in oil and have a beer.

Nuoro

Day 16 La Caletta to Sassari and the Costa Smeralda

Friday 4 October

Moving day, but before leaving I have one last view of the sea from the broad walk, and then set off back north before heading to Sassari. I planned to visit the Costa Smeralda, where David and Tina have a house at Elephant Beach, and where we stayed in 2005. The port area of Olbia, which you drive through on the way to the Costa, is extensive and complex, and there are large ferries. I wonder if I could across from Corsica to here rather than to Santa Teresa. There is a viewpoint that gives a view of the coast framed by distant mountains, but there is a coach and a medley of cars, and I drive past without stopping.

The quality of the streetscape and landscaping changes dramatically. I set the sat nav for Cala di Volpe, which takes me to the top of a luxurious suburban development. The quality of the roadside landscaping and walling is extraordinary. The gates of the houses seem to follow a style of

House in Costa Smeralda

Spiaggia la Celvia

Rocks between Spiaggia la Celvia and Elephant Beach

millionaire driftwood. There's lots of security. I reset google maps to a spiaggia a little east of Elephant Bay, and drive to a discrete car park and pay three euros to park.

I walk a couple of 100 yards down to the beach. The sand is coarse, which is what I remember from David and Tina's, and there are huge pink granite boulders. I walk to the end of the beach and try clambering the rocks. I'm in bare feet, and the rock is rough and sharp and I have to take care not to injure myself. I go 100 meters or so before realising it's much too far to Elephant Beach. So I return, change into my trunks and go for a dip.

It's time to head for Sassari, where I'm to leave the car and spend the night. The road is good, but for some reason, Google takes me off the main highway onto a rural road. I don't mind. It's interesting. It's very agricultural here. The western third of the island is volcanic, so maybe the soils are fertile.

Unfortunately, I haven't checked whether I've had any messages from the hotel, the Locanda Carra Manna, I just key in the address, assuming that a decent hotel would have parking. What a mistake! Google takes me into

Typical road in Costa Smeralda

Cattedrale di San Nicola, Sassari

Via al Duomo, Sassari

the town, then up towards the Duomo. So far, so good. Then it traces a route through the narrowest of roads. They are beautifully paved with granite blocks and pebbles, but they are so narrow, there is barely space to pass. At various points, there are hideous scrape marks on either side.

Finally, I make it to the Piazza Tola and park in front of a restaurant and go in and find the hotel just around the corner. It's shut so I go back to the pizzeria and order lunch and check my phone, there is a message from the hotel saying, "on no account try to get to the hotel following Google, park in the Piazza Mazzotti, and walk four minutes". I text them and say I'm here. And while I'm eating, a young woman arrives. She says, finish your lunch and come and check in.

I leave my gear and decide, since I don't need the car, that I'll drop it off now rather than wait till tomorrow. It's narrow back downhill, but not as bad as getting there. I pass a petrol station and fill up. The Noleggiare car hire is barely a kilometre or so, and I drop off the car without any drama, and catch a bus back. The driver wants the exact fare but I only have a five euro note. A man in the front seat asks how much and finds the right change, then pockets my five euros. We all have a laugh.

Room in Locana Carra Manna hotel

Via Francesco Cetti

Museo della Città Corso Vittorio Emanuele II

Ancient Fiat 500

Piazza Tola

Back at the hotel, I wash and rest. I've reserved dinner at the restaurant Liberty on the advice of my host, since it's Friday and everywhere will be booked. It's only a short walk. I'm the first guest and the restauranteur, clothed all in black with multiple tattoos. I order the fish of the day – Ombrina. It's large, almost a metre long. I know because I'm sitting opposite a glass-fronted cabinet with eight or nine fish being salted. I don't have the whole fish, of course, just a cut from a fresh sample in the kitchen, served with roasted vegetables, followed by Catalan tart then an early bed.

Restaurant Liberty Sassari

Day 17 Sassari to Porto Torres and ferry

Saturday 5 October

Saturday, there is a notice from Corsica Ferries saying that the sailing has changed from 2:30 to 8:30 which will make catching trains on Saturday challenging. I try to remain calm and not panic about missing connections. It means I will have a relaxing day in Sassari and Porto Torres.

Breakfast is impressive. The waitress brings one dish after another. I wrap up what I can't eat in a serviette for lunch. I leave my bag and go off and to explore the old city. It feels very Italian and very lived in. The streets are narrow. People hang out chatting. There is washing drying overhead. Cafes with the clientele in heated discussion. It's Saturday, and there's a holiday feel to the day.

I enter the Chiesa di Santa Caterina, the Palazzio Ducal and the Pinacoteca Nazionale. The Marie looks swanky and there are chic Italian

Palazzo Ducale Sassari Piazza del Comune

women chatting with smartly dressed men around big flash cars. I go into the Duomo, the Cattedrale di San Nicola. Churches have a peaceful, calming effect and I sit in a pew at the back and contemplate the vaulting and the altar.

I walk through the Piazza Del Castillo and the Piazza Italia looking at the palaces and trees and noting the people passing by and bump into the same parties of tourists at different places. There is a police presence, young, tough men in tight jodhpurs and shiny boots, motorbike cops and other local police. There was a Forza Italia sign and a knot of people chatting, perhaps there's to be a political rally. There's a statue of Victor Emmanuel II, king of Sardinia from 1849-1861, who then became the first king of a united Italy. He looks short, grumpy and very self-important. The plume of his helmet looks like a pigeon has landed on his head. There's an archeology site, and three or four meters below the current street level, one can see signs of the old Roman city.

I found the Healthy Garden restaurant and order an orange, carrot and lemon smoothy. It's delicious and reviving, but I've used all my change, and I'm worried that the bus driver to Torres will need the exact fare. So I

Pinacoteca Nazionale Piazza Santa Caterina

retrace my steps to another very Italian cafe. It's full and the patrons are loud and effusive. There are pictures of football teams on the wall and team colours and there are various groups of men having animated discussions.

I order cappuccino and eat the sweets I pinched from the hotel reception. I offer one to a little boy who was running about, but he refuses, presumably, his parents have told him never to accept anything from strange old men. I return to the hotel and retrieve my rucksack and set off for the bus station. I nearly come to grief when I step off the curb without looking, but luckily, all is well, and I have just enough time to buy a bus ticket at the cafe, so I didn't need to worry about paying

I am bowling along to Porto Torres and ruminate about how if one had done one's homework and knew what one was doing, it would be possible to explore almost all of Sardinia, including the mountain villages and beach resorts, by bus. Nevertheless, it was convenient having the car and I would have had to do things differently by bus, which will probably have required more time. The driver drops me outside the maritime terminal. I seem to have lost my iPhone charging cable, and only have 13%

Piazza D'Italia and statue of Vittorio Emanuele II

left on my phone's battery. I text Scharlie to let her know.

The terminal is deserted. After all, I'm early. There's a cafe and a sign saying deposito bagagli, so for five euros, the proprietor takes my bag and leaves me free to wander. I'm a 100 yards down the road when I think to ask him if I can charge my phone. He says, fine. I wander around the Marina appraising and admiring the fishing fleet. Some of the boats have three dinghies with lights aboard. I've seen them fishing at night with a big bag net. The small boats stretch out the net and attract the fish with the lights. Gradually, the net is drawn in and the bag tightens.

The nets are laid out in long lines on the concrete top of the wharf to dry. One of the boats has washing drying, and a Vietnamese looking sailor emerges to retrieve his dry clothes. There are also small, ancient boats with stepped masts and small inboard engines. They're small, narrow and elegant. Maybe they don't go out as far as the bigger boats. There are also an assortment of yachts and power boats, but these are less interesting.

I walk along to the curving mole, but there is broken glass and syringes, so I turn back and walk to the park in front of the small spiaggia and stop on a bench and eat the lunch I have saved from breakfast. From there, I

Corsica/Sardinia Ferry approaching Porto Torres landing

wander back to the terminal for a pee and then go in search of the Roman ruins to the west of the terminal. The bath houses are impressive, with tile floors and watercourses still visible. The museum closes at four, so it's too late to spend more time there and I wander back to the Piazza Garibaldi, where there is a cafe in the sunshine and I order a drink and watch the world go by. I feel sorry for the black hawkers with their trolleys of goods, sorry for how they're either ignored or dismissed. How on earth do they survive? Do they regret coming here? What future can they anticipate?

I'm lightheaded after my drink and head back to the terminal and retrieve my bag and settle down to write my journal. It's still quiet. Two hours till we sail. I've checked in, though and everything seems in order, so no worries. However, there is further delay, and we don't set off until 10:30pm. The crossing is remarkably comfortable. This is a huge ship, and once on in the cabin, in the centre, there is no sense of movement. The cabin is spacious and the bed and pillow deliciously soft, and I drop off immediately.

Double berth car deck

Day 18 Toulon to Marseille

Sunday 6 October

I'm awake at seven with an announcement on the Tannoy, and for a moment think we may be docking early and I might catch my trains, I shower, dress and go up to the Panorama Bar on deck nine and see that we are approaching land, but still have a long way to go. Dawn is emerging. The horizon is tinged pink with the dark hills behind. I go back and pack and leave my bag while I go in search of a coffee.

The cafes on the fifth floor are crowded and there is a long queue, so I return to the Panorama Bar and order a petite déjeuner with croissant of fresh orange juice, which tastes delicious and gets me thinking that I should squeeze oranges at home, and maybe I'll buy a citrus press when I get back.

We entered the inner harbour. There is a barrage stretching across the

Entering Toulon

mouth a meter above the water and there are ancient fortifications and various grey and lethal looking warships. There is a wait to disembark, then I'm off to the station. It's about a 20 minute walk, but it's most pleasant, and I'm in no rush now as I've missed my train.

First along the promenade and then into the old town of Toulon via the Cour de Lafayette. There's a street market in progress down the middle of the pedestrianised avenue. It's tree lined and delightful. The stalls, of which there are hundreds stretching a mile or more, are laden with brightly coloured fruit and vegetables, fish, artisan bread, olives and many other delicious-looking food stuffs.

I see a sign for iPhone doctor and buy a charger for my phone for 15 euros, a real bargain. At the rail station, I can get to Marseille, but my phone tells me that all the trains on to Lille today are full. I take the slow train along the coast from Toulon to Marseille and get a chance to see the delights of the Cote d'Ivoire – villas clustered amongst the trees on rocky slopes. It's green and verdant, not the dry landscape of Sardinia. My suspicions are confirmed. There are no trains today, so I book on the 6:04 tomorrow morning.

Street market Cour Lafayette

Day 19 Marseille to home

Monday 7 October

I book a room in the Holiday Inn just over the road from the station since I'm forced to spend the night in Marseille. I went for a light meal in an Exki cafe. It's a chain, but it's making a real effort to be healthy, sustainable with fresh, complex ingredients and recyclable packaging and cutlery.

Back at the hotel and sit in the lounge till I can check-in at two. I manage to change my Eurostar booking and book a new ticket to Hathersage. With luck. I'll get in about 5:30pm. I'm in bed early, having seen very little of Marseille, but having successfully rearranged my onward travel Monday.

An early start and a queue for coffee and croissant then the TGV to Paris. It is still dark, but the train is relatively empty, and we are bowling along at 370 kilometres an hour. The Metro in Paris is the stuff of

Cour Lafayette

nightmares, and the Gare du Lyon and the Gare Du Nord are huge and confusing. There is a long queue for the ticket machine. You can't just tap your bank card, and it took a while to find the right ticket. But finally, I was on the train to Lille and caught up on my sleep and was able to buy a nice lunch. At the baggage check the police asked if I had a knife. Yes, I said, thinking, sadly, I'm going to lose my trusty knife I bought in Fairbanks, Alaska. I got out the dry bag from the top of my sock and handed it over. He found the knife, opened it, measured it against his hand, then said to his mate it has a button and handled it back. I said, thank you most relieved. The rest of the journey passed without incident.

Place Albert Gare de Toulon

Eurostar St Pancras

Mother Goddess from Cuccuru s'Arrius, Cabras

ITINERARY

Day	Date	Start	Finish	Km	Miles	Ascent m	Accommodation	Star
Thu	19-Sep	Hathersage	London				Comfy Euston	***
Fri	20-Sep	London	Marseille/Ile Rousse				Ferry	***
Sat	21-Sep	Ile Rousse/Calenza	Bonifatu	11.5	7	560	Auberge de la Fôret	***
Sun	22-Sep	Bonifatu	Mansu	15	9	800	Chez Veronique	***
Mon	23-Sep	Tuarelli	Galéria	12.8	8	230	U Filipaghju	***
Tue	24-Sep	Galéria	Girolata	11.5	7	770	Le Cormoran	***
Wed	25-Sep	Girolata	Curzu	10.5	7	840	Gite de Curzo	***
Thu	26-Sep	Curzu	Serriera	8	5	440	Gite L'Alivi	***
Fri	27-Sep	Serriera	Ota	10.8	7	1050	Chez Marie	***
Sat	28-Sep	Ota	Evisa/ Cargese	10	7	650	Hotel Saint Jean	***
Sun	29-Sep	Cargese	Cargese			1225	Hotel Saint Jean	***
Mon	30-Sep	Cargese	Bonifacio/Santa Teresa				Angelique	***
Tue	01-Oct	Santa Teresa	La Caletta				Fronte Mare	***
Wed	02-Oct	La Calaetta	Oliena				Fronte Mare	***
Thu	03-Oct	La Caletta	Talana Blue Zone				Fronte Mare	***
Fri	04-Oct	La Caletta	Sassari				Locanda Carra Mani	***
Sat	05-Oct	Sassari	Porto Torres				Ferry	***
Sun	06-Oct	Toulon	Marseille				Holiday Inn	***
	07-Oct	Marseille	London/Home				Home	

KIT LIST

Item	Make	Model	Notes	No.	Weight gm	Stars
Rucksack	Lightwave	Fastpac 30	Excellent, durable but very light.	1	992	***
Rucksac cover	Lowe			1	63	**
Silk Liner	Sea to Summit	Mummy		1	138	***
First aid kit	Boots		Good, added compeed, second skin, arnica,	1	250	***
Note book	Moleskin		I always use these for my journals	1	111	***
Pens	Biro		Excellent	2	22	***
Phone	iPhone	12	Good battery life, excellent camera	1	75	***
Head torch	Petzl	Light	and spare battery	1	36	***
Maps	Didier Richard	Corse du Nord	Excellent, accurate, durable and easy to use	2	46	***
Compass	Silva	with whistle	Excellent, very practical, have always used Silva	1	42	***
Reading glasses				1	22	***
Pocket knife	Gerber	Paraframe		1	54	***
Debit card			Essential	1	1	
Dry bags	Sea to Summit	Assorted	Excellent, durable and completely waterproof	5	310	***
Walking poles	Black Diamond	Distance flz	Excellent, light and well balanced	2	384	***
Sandals	Clogs		Useful for tired feet and getting into water	1	296	**
Water bottle	HydraPak 1L			1	100	**
Pee bottle	Nalgene 1L			1	112	***
Sun cream	SunSense	Factor 50		1	30	
Toothbrush	CuraProX			1	25	
Towel	Mountain Warehouse	Ex Large	Plus mini Go face towel	2	151	**
Lenses, spectacles				1	90	
TOTAL KIT					3,350	
Boots	Sportiva		Wide fitting replacement boots bought in Corte	1	890	***
Gaiters	Sea to Summit		Good, light	1	110	**
Anorak	Arcteryx	Alpha SV	Orange	1	506	***
Fleece	Berghaus		Windproof with hood	1	518	***
Cap	North Face			1	86	**
Pants			Excellent, fit well and good pockets	1	351	***
Shorts	Kühl		Excellent, fit well and good pockets	1	299	***
Shorts						
T shirts	Adidas		Excellent, stayed looking smart	3	450	***
Leggings	Lowe		Gite wear	1	20	***
Socks	Bridgedale		Excellent, very comfortable	3	0	
Underpants	M&S			3	46	
Swimming trunks	Speedo			1	90	***
Belt	Jukmo	Ratchet belt	Essential, because you loose weight (6-7 kilos)	1	25	***
TOTAL CLOTHES					3,391	
TOTAL					6,741	
Clothes bag					1715	

TRAINING WALKS

Date	Name	Mileage	Km	Ht ft	Time hrs
04/01/22	High Cup Nick North Pennines	7.2	5.4	1590	5
05/01/22	High Force Teesdale	5.0	12.5	900	3.5
12/01/22	Spurn Head Lincolnshire	7.2	11.8	72	5
14/01/22	Caistor circular Lincolnshire Wolds	5.0	11.0	346	4
22/01/22	Sandy Bay Iona	2.5	15.7	100	2
23/01/22	St Columba's Bay and Marble Quarry Iona	5.5	16.9	610	5
08/02/22	Dun I and North Coast Iona	7.0	17.7	700	6
09/02/22	Aberffraw Anglesey	3.0	8.0	646	2.5
10/02/22	Cambrian Way Barmouth	7.0	17.7	2141	6
23/02/22	Cadar Idris Dolgellau	5.4	5.2	2508	5
09/03/22	Stanage	4	6.4	300	2
	Total	59	95	9,913	46

www.ingramcontent.com/pod-product-compliance
Lightning Source LLC
Chambersburg PA
CBHW041623220426
43662CB00001B/26